BOY SCOUTS OF AMERICA
MERIT BADGE SERIES

SALESMANSHIP

"Enhancing our youths' competitive edge through merit badges"

BOY SCOUTS OF AMERICA®

Requirements

1. Do the following:

    a. Explain the responsibilities of a salesperson and how a salesperson serves customers and helps stimulate the economy.

    b. Explain the differences between a business-to-business salesperson and a consumer salesperson.

2. Explain why it is important for a salesperson to do the following:

    a. Research the market to be sure the product or service meets the needs of customers.

    b. Learn all about the product or service to be sold.

    c. If possible, visit the location where the product is built and learn how it is constructed. If a service is being sold, learn about the benefits of the service to the customer.

    d. Follow up with customers after their purchase to confirm their satisfaction and discuss their concerns about the product or service.

3. Write and present a sales plan for a product or service and a sales territory assigned by your counselor.

4. Make a sales presentation of a product or service assigned by your counselor.

5. Do ONE of the following and keep a record (cost sheet). Use the sales techniques you have learned, and share your experience with your counselor:

    a. Help your unit raise funds through sales of merchandise or of tickets to a Scout event.

- b. Sell your services such as lawn raking or mowing, pet watching, dog walking, snow shoveling, and car washing to your neighbors. Follow up after the service has been completed and determine the customer's satisfaction.
- c. Earn money through retail selling.

6. Do ONE of the following:
   a. Interview a salesperson and learn the following:
      1. What made the person choose sales as a profession?
      2. What are the most important things to remember when talking to customers?
      3. How is the product or service sold?
      4. Include your own questions.
   b. Interview a retail store owner and learn the following:
      1. How often is the owner approached by a sales representative?
      2. What good traits should a sales representative have? What habits should the sales representative avoid?
      3. What does the owner consider when deciding whether to establish an account with a sales representative?
      4. Include at least two of your own questions.

7. Investigate and report on career opportunities in sales, then do the following:
   a. Prepare a written statement of your qualifications and experience. Include relevant classes you have taken in school and merit badges you have earned.
   b. Discuss with your counselor what education, experience, or training you should obtain so you are prepared to serve in a sales position.

Contents

What Salespeople Do. 7

Research a Product or Service 11

Build a Solid Relationship With Customers. 15

Develop a Top-Notch Sales Plan. 21

A Winning Sales Presentation 25

Time to Sell. 29

Interview a Professional. 38

Sales Career Opportunities. 41

Salesmanship Resources 47

What Salespeople Do

Sales can offer a challenging and rewarding career for those who enjoy interacting with people from all walks of life. Self-confidence, motivation, friendliness, and the persistence necessary to overcome obstacles and solve problems—all of these are important traits for people who choose sales as a career.

Top sales professionals know that customers who trust them will buy again. They realize these customers will spread the word about the positive experience they had, including news about the courtesy and friendliness of the salesperson and the quality of the product.

Responsibilities of Sales Professionals

Salespeople have important responsibilities to the company or organization they represent and to the customers they serve. These responsibilities include:

- Having in-depth knowledge of and showing support for the quality of the product or service

- Learning and practicing sound sales techniques that offer a win/win outcome for the company and the customers

- Valuing and building excellent long-term relationships with customers

- Representing the company honorably through high moral character and straightforward actions

- Preserving public trust by dealing with people fairly and honestly, and by solving problems quickly and to the customer's satisfaction

- Promoting economic growth through sales

> Good salespeople practice a straightforward philosophy: If you are friendly and honest, people will buy from you.

Service to Customers

Salespeople's most important duty is to serve customers in the same way they would like to be served if the shoe were on the other foot. A professional, well-groomed appearance, direct eye contact, a winning smile, a courteous and kind manner, and an open-minded approach to assisting people on their own terms are crucial ways that salespeople can best serve their customers.

Customers buy when they feel confident that the purchase meets their needs, especially when it comes to big-ticket items like cars and homes. To motivate a customer to buy, all lingering doubts must be met by the salesperson's ability to listen to, focus on, and straightforwardly address the customer's concerns.

When customers feel comfortable with their reasons for making a purchase, sales follow. In turn, sales stimulate economic growth, not only of the salesperson's bank account but also of our communities and society.

The Hershey With a Heart

The Hershey's chocolate factory in Hershey, Pennsylvania, offers a perfect example of how product sales can promote the economic growth of the community and beyond.

Born in 1857 to a Mennonite family in rural Pennsylvania, Milton Hershey attended school through the fourth grade. He later became an apprentice to a chocolate maker and learned everything he could about the craft. At age 18, Hershey opened his first candy shop. He later opened candy businesses in Chicago, New Orleans, and New York, and the Lancaster Caramel Company in Lancaster, Pennsylvania.

Hershey with a student from the school he and his wife, Catherine, founded in 1909 for underprivileged children.

However, Hershey's heart was wrapped in chocolate, so he sold the caramel company for $1 million and used the money to build a chocolate factory near his hometown in rural Pennsylvania. It was an instant success. Countless positions and financial security—not just for factory workers, but for candy suppliers and distributors, cocoa farmers, truck drivers, construction workers, health-care workers, and many other workers in Pennsylvania and across the United States and abroad—were created by this successful business.

Hershey's employees were loyal, and he treated them well. In addition to decent wages, Hershey invested in housing, education, and health care for his employees. As the business grew, the community around it grew, too. Today, as a tourist attraction, Hershey, Pennsylvania, continues to spur broad economic growth.

Research a Product or Service

You must learn all about the product (such as shortbread cookies or video games) or service (such as lawn mowing or dog walking) before you begin selling. If practical, visit the factory where the product is made or the business is located to gain first-hand knowledge about the product or service. If that is not possible, search online (with your parent's permission) or visit a public library to find information about the company and its products, including customer comments.

Salespeople must update their knowledge as the product line expands or changes with the fluctuating marketplace. As a salesperson, you must keep up with industry trends, pricing, marketing, packaging, and other product developments.

> As a salesperson, your company's business is *your* business to know thoroughly!

Seasonal products

SALESMANSHIP 11

Questions a Salesperson Should Ask

You should be able to answer the following questions about your product or service and the organization for which you work.

PRODUCT INFORMATION

- How long has the product or service been on the market?
- Is it new or improved?
- Is it an easily recognized brand?
- Is the product seasonal (Christmas trees), a fad (something trendy that quickly fades from popularity), or a tried-and-true standard?
- Why do people need or want it? What makes the product or service different from or superior to the competition?

MARKETING

- How is the product or service marketed, and what do customers like about it?
- What claims or promises about the product or service does the company make, and are those claims provable?
- What is the downside of the product or service—what do unsatisfied customers say about it?

CUSTOMER SERVICE

- What customer service standards does the company follow before and after the sale?
- How does the company ensure customer satisfaction and repeat business?
- How have quality-control issues with the product or service been resolved?
- Can the customer return the product for a full refund?

Build a Solid Relationship With Customers

To build a relationship with customers, be attentive to friendly, respectful, and professional ways that you can help potential buyers clear hurdles toward a purchase.

Professional Skills

Personal appearance is important. A well-groomed, professional appearance from head to toe is the first thing a customer should notice about you. Be considerate and friendly, gracious and respectful. You want customers to feel comfortable talking with you.

Successful salespeople stress the importance of interpersonal skills for reaching sales goals. Use simple, clear language when talking or writing to others about the product and the sale. Your coworkers and customers will appreciate clear communication, especially if the details are complicated. Avoid jargon (slang) or highly technical language. Use simple language to describe technical terms. The more you know about the product or service you are selling, the easier it will be to describe it in simple terms.

Listening is one key to customer satisfaction. Learning about people's likes, dislikes, problems, and goals will help you sell a product or service that meets their needs. Remember to make eye contact and other friendly gestures, such as nodding, to show that you are listening and are interested.

Customers appreciate punctual sales professionals who have self-discipline and initiative. If the sale involves a lot of money, the salesperson might have to meet with the customer several times to close the deal. Plan your schedule daily and

---

Always be on time for meetings, and be available to your customers when they need you, whether by phone, email, or in person. If you are running late for a meeting, call the customer immediately and explain what happened. Do not leave anyone wondering where you are.

Build a Solid Relationship With Customers

weekly, making sure you write down important information about when to make introductory calls, callbacks, and follow-up calls.

When negotiation becomes complicated or difficult, a salesperson must be able to handle the situation—however stressful—with consistent tact, diplomacy, and persistence. Even customers who act discourteously should be treated tactfully. Staying calm and polite often will have a reassuring effect and may enable you to politely carry on with business. Never lose your cool with a customer, no matter how badly the interaction goes. If you do find your temper rising—which can happen if the customer becomes angry or makes unreasonable demands—excuse yourself for a minute. Leave the room and take 10 deep breaths to relax before returning.

Build a Solid Relationship With Customers

Your tone should always convey enthusiasm for the product or service, your company, and the customer. Honesty in all your dealings also is crucial. Nothing destroys buyer confidence faster than a salesperson who breaks a promise or misrepresents the qualities of a product or service.

Customer Follow-Through

Following up with customers is one of the most crucial skills of salesmanship. Why? Think of your customers as a loyal base of friends who can help you increase sales, spread goodwill about you and your company, and guide improvements to your business strategy.

Customers welcome the chance to share their opinions about a product or service they purchased, and they appreciate that the salesperson cared to ask. You are likely to get good feedback, even if it is negative, once customers have purchased the product and had a chance to try it out.

Make every effort to fulfill an unsatisfied customer's needs in an efficient, quiet, and confident manner. This is your chance to practice super salesmanship—to leap over tall obstacles and find practical solutions to any and all problems. Any negative feedback requires further follow-up once you have addressed the customer's concerns. More often than not, customers will appreciate your determination and honesty when you have made the effort to solve problems to their satisfaction.

Build a Solid Relationship With Customers

Once you have a satisfied customer, don't be afraid to ask for future business: "I hope you will think of me the next time you need your dog walked, and please recommend my service to your friends."

When you start to get repeat customers and recommendations, consider other personal ways to keep in touch. For example, send loyal customers a holiday or birthday card annually, or offer free samples or discounts on future goods. Try any number of attractive deals to show that you value your customers' continued business.

Many salespeople, particularly those who sell expensive items such as automobiles and houses, work on *commission*. When they make a sale, they receive a percentage of the total sales price. They do not make a regular salary. Rather, they rely on their sales skills to provide income. A salaried salesperson receives a salary or hourly pay. Many salespeople who work in department stores receive a steady paycheck. In general, salaried employees do not earn a commission on sales made.

BUILD A SOLID RELATIONSHIP WITH CUSTOMERS

A **sales quota** is a goal set by the company that the sales representative must try to meet. For example, a person in tractor sales might have to sell eight tractors per month to meet the sales quota. If the salesperson consistently meets the quota over the course of a year, the company might offer rewards like cash bonuses or free travel.

Gumball Guy

A medical supply salesperson built his business in hospitals and doctors offices throughout North Carolina by bringing a jar filled with gumballs to clients on his first sales visit. Each time he returned to sell medical supplies, he brought gumballs to refill the jar. Even if he did not make a sale that day, he refilled the jar. Doctors and nurses so looked forward to his visits that they wound up buying all of their standard supplies from one salesperson—the "gumball guy!"

SALESMANSHIP   19

Develop a Top-Notch Sales Plan

To develop a top-notch sales plan for your product or service, start by writing down your thoughts. Describe your business and the product or service. Then write down details about the market—the specific group of people—you are targeting.

Next, write down your sales strategy. Decide how you plan to market your product—by advertising, word-of-mouth, mail, phone, or the internet, for instance. Perhaps you can think of an unusual sales hook or a catchy slogan to increase product or service awareness and recognition. Give your sales strategy careful thought, because it will set the course for your business.

Consider your competitors—who else offers the same product or service you do? Identify how your product or service stacks up to the competition, how it is similar to and different from your competition. Think of how you can reach that portion of the market that your competitors do not.

Identify the exact territory in which you will sell your product or service. If you are starting a neighborhood business, you might want to include a local map with your sales plan that shows the area where you live and your specific plans for canvassing the territory to create sales. This can mean going door-to-door (with a buddy) or sending a brochure to each person in your neighborhood.

Compare the price of your product or service to that of competitors. If you charge $35 for mowing an average yard, check the prices of other lawn mowing services in your area.

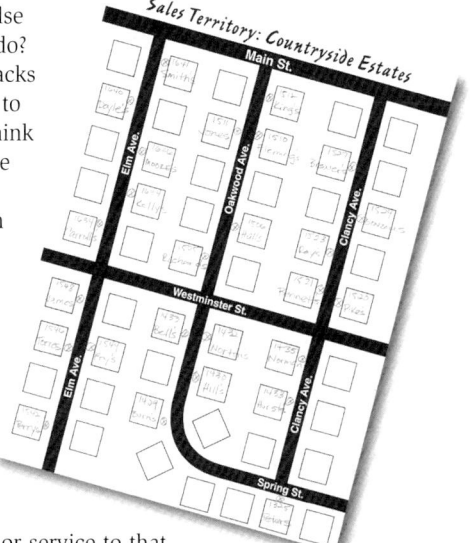

sales territory.
An area assigned to a salesperson by his or her employer. The area can cover a large geographical area.

SALESMANSHIP

Before you develop a sales plan, check local laws and obtain any permits or insurance required to advertise and conduct business in your sales territory.

Customer	Service	Yard Size	Rate	Our Rate
B. Jefferson	Green Thumb	1,700 sq. ft.	$25	$25
S. Maynard	Shorty's	1,500 sq. ft.	$25	$20
L. Nguyen	Green Thumb	1,800 sq. ft.	$30	$25
B. Pearson	Steve R.	1,200 sq. ft.	$20	$20
A. Drake	Green Thumb	2,300 sq. ft.	$35	$35
D. Cooke	Cutting Edge	900 sq. ft.	$20	$15

How much will it cost you to buy, or at least maintain, your equipment? Will you need a truck or special vehicle to transport your equipment? How about hidden costs such as gasoline and oil for the mowing equipment and transportation? Write it all down, and be realistic about your expenses.

You might be able to attract customers by offering a slightly lower rate for your service than competitors charge, or by providing every 10th lawn mowing for free. Your competitors might have a similar strategy, so stay on your toes. Be prepared to adjust your sales strategy to meet market demands.

Remember to detail the bottom-line costs of creating and selling your product or service. If you sell Christmas ornaments and it costs you $1 apiece for the materials and 25 cents more per item to market them, carefully consider the selling price that will allow you to make a profit. Be particularly careful with seasonal items—you don't want to get stuck with unsold inventory when the season ends. It is easy to underestimate costs, especially as you start your own business. Estimate all expenses, and always pad your budget a bit, just in case.

Estimate your profits only after you have created a realistic list of your expenses. Be very conservative with your profit estimates. You never know when a quality-control problem or market fluctuation might pop up and quickly eat away your business.

> Your time is valuable. Consider a fair wage for your time and for the type of work you are doing, and add that to your list of expenses. Be careful that the amount of time you spend is not worth more than your expected earnings. Measure the amount of time it takes to do the work. If you spend so much time working that it diminishes your profits, find ways to streamline your tasks.

Sales Phenomenon Michael S. Dell

Some people might say Michael S. Dell is a natural salesperson. The founder and chief executive officer of Dell Computer Corporation started his amazing career when he was a preteen. By age 12, he had already made $2,000 through a stamp auction. At age 16, Dell was selling newspaper subscriptions to the *Houston Post*. After noticing that his best customers were new homeowners and recently married people, he hired friends to obtain names from local marriage licenses and home mortgages. Instead of cold-calling customers to meet his sales quota, Dell focused on the people on his list. In just a year, he earned $18,000 selling newspapers—a remarkable accomplishment.

Like many young entrepreneurs, Dell was not content to rest on his laurels. As a freshman in college, he became fascinated with personal computers. A hands-on guy, he took them apart and reassembled them using better components, often adding more memory and enhanced features. When he realized that components to build a computer could be purchased for less than $1,000 and that retail stores were then selling computers for $3,000, Dell decided to build his own and compete with stores by selling his product directly to customers. He aimed to provide fast, direct service.

The innovative sales plan worked, and his new business proved very profitable. Dell reportedly earned tens of thousands of dollars a month that first year. Despite his parents' objections, Dell quit college in 1984 at the end of his freshman year to found Dell Computer Corporation. It was the first company to sell personal computers direct to customers, bypassing the middleman—in this case, retail stores. It also was the first computer company to offer next-day, on-site customer support services—Dell customers received in-home repair services.

Today, Michael Dell is the chair and chief executive officer of Dell Computer and is one of the world's wealthiest people.

A Winning Sales Presentation

Y&E: The Magazine for Teen Entrepreneurs* suggests the following checklist to guide you through the steps of planning and delivering a winning sales presentation.

STEP 1: Set a goal for your presentation.
- ☐ Determine who your customer is (in this case, your counselor) and where you will meet.
- ☐ Set a controlling purpose. What do you want the customer to do?
- ☐ Brainstorm a list of ideas and facts you want to communicate.

STEP 2: Create the presentation.
- ☐ Develop a friendly introduction that tells who you are.
- ☐ Briefly introduce your product and explain several important features.
- ☐ Explain the important ways your product improves life for the customer.
- ☐ Explain why your product is better than others.
- ☐ State the price and/or make a special offer.
- ☐ Write a sentence that asks the customer to make a buying decision.
- ☐ Gather samples or visual aids to show as you speak.
- ☐ Prepare a flier or brochure to give to the potential customer.

STEP 3: Practice the delivery.
- ☐ Read your presentation aloud into a tape recorder, then listen to the recording and improve rough spots.
- ☐ Begin memorizing the presentation, and practice in front of a mirror until you feel confident.

*Source: *Y&E: The Magazine for Teen Entrepreneurs*, January/February 2001, ©2001 Ewing Marion Kauffman Foundation and KidsWay Inc. Used with permission. All rights reserved.

A Winning Sales Presentation

- ☐ Try out your presentation on a family member. If possible, have someone videotape your presentation.
- ☐ Have your family ask you questions that a customer might ask.
- ☐ Keep practicing until your presentation feels natural and spontaneous.

STEP 4: Deliver the presentation.
- ☐ Make sure you have your props and visuals.
- ☐ Dress appropriately for the business.
- ☐ Be on time.
- ☐ Shake hands and smile when you meet your customer (counselor).
- ☐ Speak slowly and observe the customer to see if you are communicating.
- ☐ Pause occasionally and ask if the customer has any questions.
- ☐ Don't panic if you forget something. You can say it later.
- ☐ Give out your marketing materials and be prepared to take the order.

The following tips for a successful sales presentation come from C. J. Hayden, a business coach, speaker, and author.

Establish rapport. Whether you are presenting to one person (your counselor) or a large group, introduce yourself and get to know a little bit about the audience members. Chat about things you have in common or about the sequence of events that brought you together.

Determine the customer's needs. Begin by repeating what you already know about the customer's needs and then start asking questions. Your script should include all the questions you must answer to write a proposal or close a sale on the spot. Ask open-ended questions—those that require more than a simple yes or no answer—to get more information from your customer.

Explain how you can meet the customer's needs. Using the information you have just gathered, describe how you can respond to each problem or goal. Use specific examples to illustrate your explanation, such as the following: "My last customer had exactly the same challenge. I was able to . . ."

Answer questions. Find out how you are doing with the sales presentation by asking, "What else do you need to know?" Keep asking for and answering questions until the customer seems satisfied. Address any concerns one by one. Reassure the customer that you have the right solution by stating specifically how you can help.

Ask for the business. Don't leave out this step! Even if you know the customer wants to see a proposal first, is talking to other salespeople, or is not ready to make a decision, ask anyway. It is the only way to find out how close you are to making a sale. How the customer responds to this question will tell you exactly what you need to resolve before the person will buy from you.

Decide on a next step. Whether or not you closed the sale, be absolutely certain that both you and the customer know what happens next. Is the customer ready to get started? When? Will there be a contract and/or purchase order? Who has to sign it? Is a written proposal required? Does the customer want to check your references? Can you call back in a week? Be sure to ask if you can do anything to help move things forward.

For one-on-one presentations, like the one you will give to your merit badge counselor, work on your interviewing and listening skills. When you present to a group of people, your speaking skills become more important.

> "It's important for Scouts to remember selling isn't just in the business world," said Justin Hitt, a sales and marketing consultant and former member of Boy Scout Troop 1785. "They have to sell themselves in job interviews, even in their Scouting leadership roles."

Time to Sell

It is now time to put your new skills to practical use. For requirement 5, you can help your troop raise funds, sell your own services, or find work in retail sales.

Help Your Unit Raise Funds

Let's say you have decided to help your troop raise funds by selling lawn fertilizer in the spring and fall. One Dallas, Texas, Scout troop does this as its main fund-raiser each year. Here is how they do it.

The troop starts by developing a business plan that will ensure brisk sales of fertilizer. The Scouts research the product and the market, identify a sales territory, decide the best time to initiate sales and deliver the product, determine how they will market the fertilizer to customers, and discuss how they will deliver the product on time.

RESEARCH THE PRODUCT

The Scouts research the retail price of fertilizer in local stores and compare that to the bulk wholesale price the Scouts will pay to the manufacturer. From this, the Scouts can determine how much each bag of fertilizer costs them and how much they can charge customers per bag, thereby establishing the troop's gross profit for each bag sold.

For instance, if it costs $2 per 10-pound bag to buy the fertilizer from the manufacturer, and the Scouts can sell the fertilizer in the current market for $6 per bag, and they have no other sales costs, the gross profit would be $4 per bag sold.

RESEARCH THE MARKET

The Scouts also research the benefits and selling points of the brand of fertilizer they want to sell. In this example, benefits could include lower nitrogen content, which is recommended

wholesale. Products sold in bulk to industries, banks, railroads, airlines, governments, retail stores, and other large institutions such as schools and hospitals.

TIME TO SELL

Search for "teen entrepreneurs" on the internet—with your parent's permission—and you will find hundreds of stories about young people selling everything from a secret salsa recipe to holiday gift wrapping.

for Texas lawns in April and October—exactly when Scouts will deliver the fertilizer to customers. Selling points might include telling customers that all proceeds will help the Scouts raise money for their upcoming Appalachian Trail backpacking trek, and that the fertilizer will be delivered to their doorstep.

The Scouts ask their parents to help identify potential customers among neighbors, friends, relatives, and acquaintances.

IDENTIFY SALES TERRITORIES

The troop assigns sales territories where Scouts will try to sell fertilizer. This way, the Scouts will not cover the same areas, and customers will not receive calls from more than one salesperson. The Scouts also develop a straightforward sales presentation: They state their name and troop, the product they are selling, and where the proceeds will go.

MARKET THE PRODUCT

One-page press releases are sent to local newspapers, radio stations, and weekly advertisers, and posted on community bulletin boards two weeks before the fertilizer drive. The press releases announce the sale and explain how it will help fund the local Scout troop. Contact information is prominently displayed at the top of the notices.

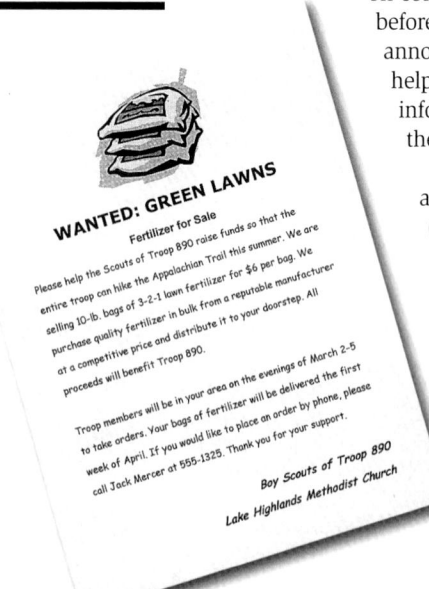

In one day, the Scouts deliver fliers all over their individual territories (neighborhoods). The flier notifies customers when Scouts will be in their area to take orders and states what troop is raising funds and for what purpose. (Some Scouts add a short handwritten note to the bottom of the flier that tells the customer when they will visit.)

At the appointed time and day, the Scouts take orders from the customers in their sales territories. They make notes of neighbors and contacts who are not home and need to be contacted again. When the deadline for taking orders arrives, the overall order is sent to the fertilizer manufacturer.

DELIVER THE PRODUCT

Scouts deliver the fertilizer on the date promised. Within three days, they follow up to thank customers for the sale and make sure they are happy with the service and product they received. At that time, the Scouts address any concerns or problems. The Scouts also politely offer to contact each customer for their fall fertilizer drive. The follow-up ends with the Scout graciously thanking the customer once again for the business.

Sell Your Own Product or Service

Many sales opportunities exist for young people—lawn mowing and pet sitting are just the tip of the iceberg. Crafts, gift baskets, website design, specialty foods, herb or organic gardening, tree trimming, house sitting, and grocery shopping are just some of the businesses teens have started and successfully run on their own.

Following up with customers shows dedication and professionalism.

If you enjoy young children, babysitting can be lucrative and fun. Be sure you look into workshops on babysitting such as those offered by the American Red Cross.

Time to Sell

Check back with your customers to evaluate their level of satisfaction. Thank each customer, solve any problems or outstanding issues, and express appreciation for the client's feedback.

First, examine your marketable skills and interests. Check around your neighborhood to identify what people need. For instance, the *Wall Street Journal** reported that Jessie Heenan, 13, of Raymore, Missouri, started a niche business in her neighborhood when she noticed many new homes under construction. Jessie saw the mess construction crews left after completing a house, so she wrote to local housing contractors with an offer to clean up after them. After securing insurance for herself—crucial to the contractors who wanted to hire her—she got work cleaning up wood scraps, drywall, and shingles, polishing fixtures, and washing windows.

Be sure to spread the word. Your goal is to have everyone associate you with your product or service. Tell everyone you know and meet who you are, what you do, and how your product or service can benefit them.

Network your way to business success: Volunteer and become a member of neighborhood or community organizations. Show that you are a hard worker and a contributor to your community. It also helps you meet more people, communicate better, become more comfortable dealing with people, and it increases word-of-mouth business.

Dog-walking could be a booming business for you, especially if you live in an area where there are dog owners who are elderly or who vacation out-of-town.

*"Teen Entrepreneurs Turn Odd Jobs Into Businesses," *Wall Street Journal*, February 13, 2000.

Customer testimonials lend credibility. If customers rave about your product or service, ask if you can quote them in your sales materials.

By following sound strategies and carefully developing your product or service, you can move quickly from market research to successful sales.

retail sales. Products purchased in bulk from wholesalers and resold to the general public.

retail sales representative. A salesperson who sells products to the public.

Earn Money Through Retail Selling

Good retail salespeople are nearly always in demand, and advancement to top-level positions can be more rapid than in most other industries. The president and corporate executives of almost all large stores started out selling.

Much more than meets the eye goes into retail selling. Whether a business succeeds lies much in the hands of the salespeople. They make the sale that brings in the money.

> A good salesperson stays alert to the customer's needs and uses imagination to fill them. The salesperson also offers friendly, sincere, and above all, honest advice.

SALESMANSHIP

CUSTOMER SERVICE

Merely waiting on a customer and ringing up a sale is not enough. A customer might need detailed information before making a purchase, or the customer might want to know the differences between products.

Service also consists of courtesy. A pleasant greeting—by name for regular customers—is a good start. Even if you are busy with another customer, a smile or nod will tell customers you will assist them as soon as possible.

Know the Merchandise

Salespeople must know their merchandise. This knowledge promotes trust and makes selling easier and more successful. A sales professional who can answer questions about the product or service can feel confident, enjoy the work, and make more sales.

TIME TO SELL

The Wizard of Watery Products

Richie Stachowski, who was 11 when he developed an underwater walkie-talkie, sold his company, Short Stack, to Wild Planet Toys for several million dollars.

Richie's sales odyssey began during a family vacation in Hawaii. He was thrilled by the amazing variety of fish he saw while snorkeling and wished he could talk about it right then with his snorkeling partner—his dad. When he learned that no simple way existed for people to talk to each other underwater, Richie started drawing designs that night in the hotel room. His goal was to create a cheap way to communicate underwater. He researched underwater acoustics, made prototypes, and eventually built Water Talkies™.

Richie pitched Water Talkies™ to a major toy retailer. He ended the presentation by using a fish tank to ask for the sale via his Water Talkie™. The retailer bit like a shark, snatching up 50,000 units. Before long, Richie sold his product to other toy stores.

First, get a general knowledge of the merchandise. Know what items are for sale or new and what items sell best. Learn where each item is located in the store. Know when store sales are advertised and what the sale prices are. Finally, learn which of the products are not available in other stores.

SALESMANSHIP

Cost Sheets and Income Statements

A cost sheet helps you track customers, the service or product and the quantity bought, the date the sale was made, when the product or service was delivered, and when you followed up and thanked customers for their business. To help improve the way you do business, the cost sheet also should note any customer suggestions, comments, and criticism you receive. Tailor the cost sheet to fit your specific product or service. One example of a cost sheet is shown here.

An overall *income statement* can be used if you start a small business, such as lawn mowing or computer repair, and you want to get a broad perspective on how your business is doing. An income statement reflects total sales revenue (income), total sales costs (expenses), and the gross profit of the business minus operating expenses, which equals the *net profit*. The example here shows an income statement for a lawn care service.

Lawns by Troop 456

Name	Address	Phone No.	Product or Service Purchased	Quantity	Total Price	Expected Delivery Date	Actual Delivery Date	Follow-Up Date	Customer Comments
Ashby	312 Maple	555-1211	Lawn mowing, edging	1	$25.00	4/26	4/26	4/28	Good job.
Clayton	4215 Hudson	555-4100	Lawn mowing, edging	1	$35.00	4/27	4/27	4/28	Nice job, thanks for being on time.
Jacoby	1920 Forest	555-7908	Lawn mowing, edging	1	$30.00	4/27	4/27	4/28	Good job, good cleanup. Yard looks good.
Watson	601 Sunset	555-0404	Lawn mowing, edging	1	$35.00	4/29	4/29	4/30	Cut grass a little shorter next time. Nice, neat job, though.
Ashby	312 Maple	555-1211	Hedge trimming, weeding	1	$40.00	5/3	5/3	5/5	Trim side yard hedge 6 inches shorter next month.
Watson	601 Sunset	555-0404	Hedge trimming, weeding	1	$55.00	5/4	5/4	5/5	Good job. Next time throw bags of weeds in large trash can.

Lawns by Troop 456

Revenue

Customer Name	Type of Service	Weekly	Monthly
Ashby	Lawn mowing and edging	$25.00	
	Hedge trimming and weeding flower beds		$40.00
Clayton	Lawn mowing and edging	$35.00	
Jacoby	Lawn mowing and edging	$30.00	
Watson	Lawn mowing and edging	$35.00	
	Hedge trimming and weeding flower beds		$55.00

Total monthly income from weekly services:		$125.00 X 4 = $500.00
Total income from monthly services:		$95.00
Total monthly income (gross profit):		$595.00

Operating Expenses

Item	Weekly	Monthly	Seasonal	Start-up
Lawn mower				$350.00
Edger/trimmer				$90.00
Electric hedge trimmer				$50.00
Hedge clipper				$30.00
Blower				$75.00
Rake				$12.00
Extension cords				$25.00
Maintenance service				
Lawn mower (two tune-ups)			$70.00	
Oil and fuel	$5.00			
Trimmer line		$4.00		
Gasoline		$6.60		
Promotional fliers (100)			$15.00	
Business cards (500)			$20.00	
Loan repayment (10 installments)		$69.52		
Total weekly operating expenses	$5.00			
Total monthly operating expenses		$80.12		
Total seasonal operating expenses			$105.00	
Subtotal of start-up expenses				$632.00
One-time cost of interest @ 10% for loan to cover start-up costs				$63.20
Total start-up expenses				$695.20
Total operating expenses, first month of operation		$190.12		
Net profit, first month of operation (gross profit minus operating expenses)		$404.88		

SALESMANSHIP   37

… INTERVIEW A PROFESSIONAL

Interview a Professional

Talking directly to someone in the field of sales can tell you more about selling than any pamphlet can. These questions will give you an idea of what selling is all about.

Questions for Sales Professionals

1. How important are reports and record keeping, and how do they help you? How much of your time does record keeping require?
2. What kind of education does sales require?
3. What kind of travel do sales positions require? In what other ways does this work affect your family life?
4. How are salespeople paid? How much financial security is there in this field?
5. What are the prospects of getting ahead quickly? How much does the average experienced salesperson earn?
6. How might you ease a customer's concerns about buying your product?
7. How would you handle a customer who is upset with you about an error your company made even when you are quite sure the mistake was on the customer's end?
8. How do you find customers? Does your sales manager tell you whom to see, or do you find them yourself?
9. What specialized sales training did you receive from your company?
10. How do you learn about the products or services you are selling?

= INTERVIEW A PROFESSIONAL

Questions for Retail Store Owners

1. What is it like working with sales representatives in your business?
2. Is the wholesale sale representative's role in retail changing?
3. Do the salespeople who service your store practice high business standards? Are they honest?
4. What do you do when products are not delivered as promised?
5. What requirements must salespeople have to work at your store? How do you pay your salespeople? What are the prospects for getting ahead?
6. What do you rely upon most when making an ordering decision?
7. Let's say you are a good customer of and have a good relationship with a particular sales representative. What would you do if a competitor approached you with a strong bid for your business at a lower price?
8. When is the best time for a sales representative to contact you?
9. If something is wrong with an order you received, do you contact the company or the sales representative who took the order?
10. With what types of salespeople—both those you employ and those from whom you buy—are you most comfortable?

manufacturer's sales representative. Someone who works for a company that manufactures products (a wholesaler) and who sells products in bulk to businesses.

SALESMANSHIP 39

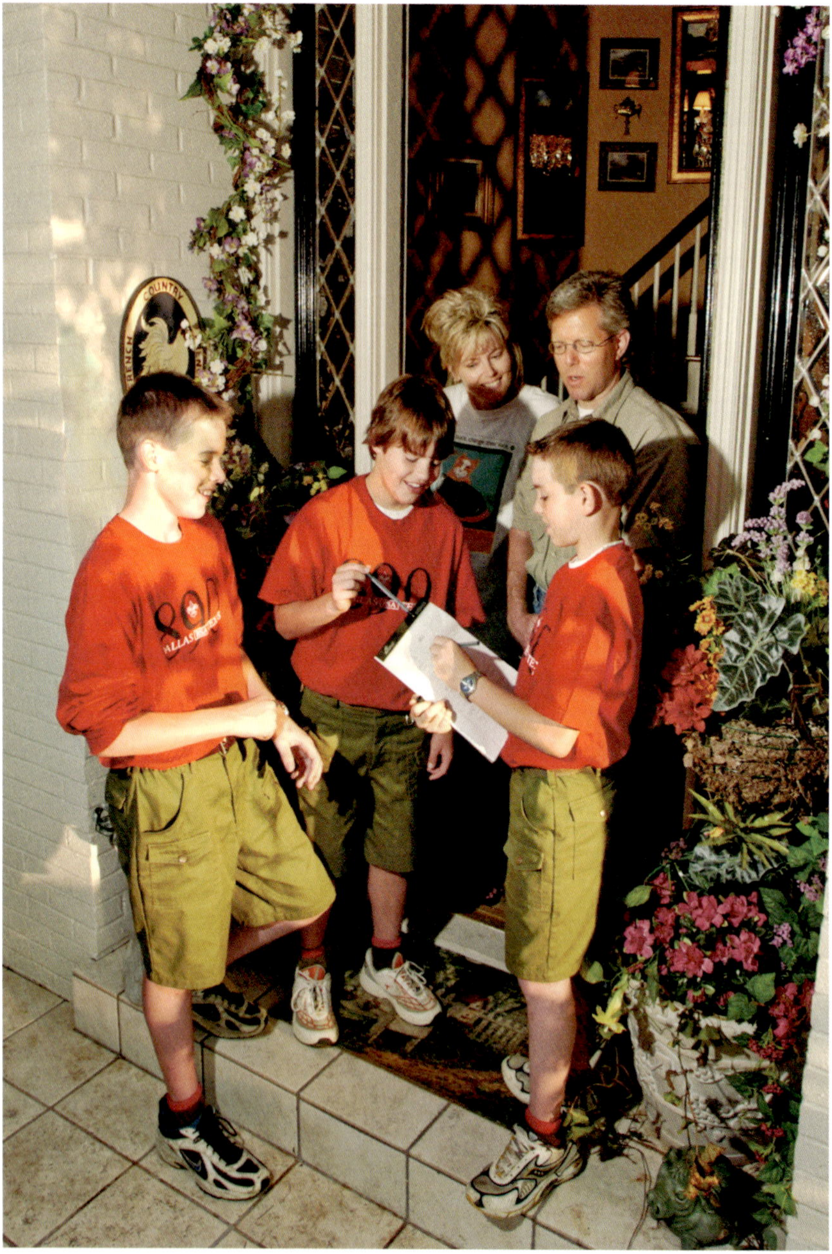
COUNTRY

Sales Career Opportunities

As you research sales career opportunities, check the classified ads in the newspaper. Notice how many positions are sales-based and how many different types of products and services people sell. In a free-enterprise society like the United States, selling is the fundamental way business gets done.

Now think about your favorite products and services, such as a favorite brand of athletic shoes or type of jeans. Pick a company you particularly like or a brand name that you always buy. Research that company on the internet (with your parent's permission) or at your local library. Find out what you can about the company, its philosophy, and its products. Focusing on a particular company or product line that you like and researching sales career opportunities within that business will make it easier for you to tailor a statement of qualifications and experience.

Education and Training

Many high schools and junior colleges offer courses in cooperation with local businesses. Under these programs, a student attends school for half a day and spends the other half working. Not only do students get on-the-job training, but they also receive regular wages for their work.

Many professional salespeople have college degrees in business. As sales techniques and the purchasing methods of consumers become more sophisticated, a well-rounded education in and knowledge of basic business practices gain importance, too.

> Summer sales positions provide valuable experience that many companies seek when hiring for career sales positions. Many firms offer special summer programs to introduce young people to sales and marketing.

Sales Career Opportunities

By looking at the rankings and then researching the top schools that offer business degrees, Scouts who are considering sales careers can select the right school for them.

The best place to start researching college-level business programs is one of the independently published college guides. Numerous guides are published each year, and they are great resources for researching colleges and finding specialized degree programs within the field of business. Online degree programs also offer an array of sales-related specialties.

U.S. News publishes *America's Best Colleges* annually. It ranks the country's top undergraduate business programs by asking deans and senior faculty members at business colleges to rate the quality of all programs on a scale of 1 (marginal) to 5 (distinguished). All the schools have programs accredited by the Association to Advance Collegiate Schools of Business.

Peterson's Four-Year Colleges features an amazing range of college programs, such as marketing operations and management, business systems networking and telecommunications, and business economics. A handful of the colleges listed offer specialized sales operations degrees. Related career fields of interest to Scouts might include advertising, communications, and public relations.

Preparing a Written Statement of Your Qualifications

A written statement of your qualifications and experience should start like any good resume, with your name, address, phone number, and email address at the top left. Type your written statement to give it a professional look.

Then state your objective. Be only as specific as you want here. If your goal or objective for the purpose of this merit badge is "to secure a high-paying position as a sales representative for GeeWhiz Cellular," then state your specific goal. If your objective is "to pursue a sales career," then state this as your broad goal.

With the list of marketable skills and your sales career goal in mind, write down the relevant classes you have taken and merit badges you have earned. For instance, if you have taken math classes that taught you how to figure percentages, multiply, subtract, add, and divide, jot them down. If you have taken a class in public speaking or served on committees at school or in your troop where speaking or leadership skills were used, record that, too. Merit badges you could mention include Personal Management, American Business, Entrepreneurship, Public Speaking, Communications, and any other badges that might help you pursue a sales career.

John Drew
124 Marshland Lane
Savannah, GA 12345

Telephone: 123-456-7890
E-mail: jdrew@scoutuniverse.net

Objective
To secure a sales representative position with Tarantula Computer Games, the most innovative video game developer in the United States.

Education
Classes in business math and algebra; two years of computer science courses, including computer programming; and excellent written and oral communication skills (3.5 GPA in English). Currently a high school sophomore, and planning to seek a bachelor's degree in business at the University of Pennsylvania.

Organizations
Boy Scouts of America, Troop 101, 2000–03. Earned Scouting merit badges in Entrepreneurship, American Business, and Public Speaking. Chaired a troop committee that planned, organized, and executed an annual spaghetti supper fund-raiser.

Skills and Experience
- Developed a computer game using the C programming language. The game won first place in the Archer High School science fair.
- Achieved expert-level play on all 10 of Tarantula Computer Games' best-sellers. Ranked fourth statewide on "BlottoBlaster," the company's hottest product.
- Organized a monthly computer game night for Cub Scout Pack 213.
- Served as freshman class treasurer at Archer High School. Used a spreadsheet to track financial records, counted and distributed funds, and made bank deposits.
- Friendly, outgoing, and honest. I enjoy working with people.
- Enthusiastic and self-motivated.
- Held several leadership roles in my Scout troop (senior patrol leader, troop historian, scribe); helped organize campouts, weekly meetings, and annual trips.

List organizations to which you belong (such as the Boy Scouts of America) and any volunteer, committee, or fund-raising work you have done. List your work history, including odd jobs and even routine household chores you perform for an allowance.

Last, discuss the college-level education or training you will need to pursue a sales career. Select a college with a business program to investigate further, and describe what you will need to do to apply. Or, describe the training you will need to serve in the position of your choice.

Look under "Objective" on the sample resume in this chapter for an example of a written statement detailing qualifications and experience.

Marketable Skills

The following are important basic skills for sales professionals:

- Excellent listening skills and an ability to communicate effectively and positively in public, on the phone, and in writing
- Organizational skills, such as the ability to keep records, remember customer names, and keep track of appointments and various stages of selling
- Math and analytical skills for figuring percentages, profits, and sales quotas, and for solving problems
- Honesty, enthusiasm, reliability, and sound judgment in financial dealings
- A positive attitude and the ability to take rejection in stride
- Drive, energy, determination, and a strong motivation to complete projects on time and within budget
- An entrepreneurial spirit and willingness to take calculated risks in pursuit of high earning potential

SALESMANSHIP 45

vegetab
grow a beautiful
Since 1964
Flowers
& Herbs
Select your favorites today

Salesmanship Resources

Scouting Literature

Boy Scout Journal; American Business, Communication, Entrepreneurship, Inventing, Personal Management, and Public Speaking merit badge pamphlets

> With your parent's permission, visit the Boy Scouts of America's official retail website, www.scoutshop.org, for a complete listing of all merit badge pamphlets and other helpful Scouting materials and supplies.

Books

Adams, Rob, and Terry Adams. *Success for Less: 100 Low-Cost Businesses You Can Start Today.* Entrepreneur Media, 1999.

Bochner, Arthur, and Rose Bochner. *The New Totally Awesome Business Book for Kids,* 3rd ed. Newmarket Press, 2009.

Brescoll, James, and Ralph M. Dahm. *Opportunities in Sales Careers.* VGM Career Horizons, 2001.

Chatzky, Jean. *Not Your Parents' Money Book: Making, Saving, and Spending Your Own Money.* Simon & Schuster Books for Young Readers, 2010.

Girard, Joe, and Stanley H. Brown. *How to Sell Anything to Anybody.* Fireside, 2006.

Godfrey, Neale S. *Neale S. Godfrey's Ultimate Kids' Money Book.* Simon & Schuster Books for Young Readers, 2002.

Joachim, Jean C. *Beyond the Bake Sale: The Ultimate School Fund-Raising Book.* St. Martin's Griffin, 2003.

Schiffman, Stephan. *25 Sales Skills They Don't Teach at Business School.* Adams Media, 2002.

Organizations and Websites

The BizWorld Foundation
555 12th St., 5th floor
Oakland, CA 94607
Toll-free telephone: 888-424-9543
Website: www.bizworld.org

Education, Training, and Enterprise Center
Toll-free telephone: 800-963-9361
Website: www.edtecinc.com

Junior Achievement
One Education Way
Colorado Springs, CO 80906
Telephone: 719-540-8000
Website: www.ja.org

Acknowledgments

Thanks to Don Herman, founder and president of Young Entrepreneur Inc., a nonprofit educational organization "Helping Teens Turn Hobbies Into Businesses Since 1997," for background information on salesmanship techniques.

Our appreciation to C.J. Hayden, the author of *Get Clients Now!*, who contributed tips on sales presentations. (Useful sales and marketing techniques can be found at Hayden's website, www.getclier

ent's perm

Speci

Magazine

(created b

Kauffman

Inc.) for

the steps

a winnin

Thar

Scout and

a sales ar

his time

The Boy Scouts of America is grateful to the men and women serving on the National Merit Badge Subcommittee for the improvements made in updating this pamphlet.

Photo and Illustration Credits

Dell Computer Corporation, courtesy—page 23

Milton Hershey School Office of Historical Records—page 9

Shutterstock.com—cover (*handshake,* ©Saklakova; *phone,* ©Prostock-studio; *clipboard,* ©Photo Melon; *laptop,* ©Evgeny Karandaev; *lemonade stand,* ©Pixel-Shot; pages 4 (©ALPA PROD), 10 (©Monkey Business Images), 13 (©Joshua Resnick), 14 (©Aigars Reinholds), 16 (©My Lit'l Eye), 18 (©Goodluz), 19 (©Stav Tsap), 31 (*children with blocks,* ©LightField Studios), 32 (©Monkey Business

lot), and 45

ons not

roperty

Boy

rker,

24, 34,